DESTINY'S
CHILD

Mike Wilson

Published in association with The Basic Skills Agency

Hodder & Stoughton

A MEMBER OF THE HODDER HEADLINE GROUP

Copyright photographs:

Cover: Ernie Stewart/Retna

p. 3 © Alex Berliner/BEI/Rex Features; p. 7 © Dave Lewis/Rex Features;
p. 9 © Gary Friedman/LA Times; p. 15 © Sipa Press/Rex Features;
p. 23 © New Line/Everett/Rex Features; p. 27 © AP Photo/Nick Ut.

Orders: please contact Bookpoint Ltd, 130 Milton Park, Abingdon, Oxon OX14 4SB.
Telephone: (44) 01235 827720. Fax: (44) 01235 400454. Lines are open from 9.00–6.00,
Monday to Saturday, with a 24 hour message answering service. You can also order through
our website www.hodderheadline.co.uk.

British Library Cataloguing in Publication Data
A catalogue record for this title is available from the British Library

ISBN 0 340 87647 6

First Published 2003
Impression number   10 9 8 7 6 5 4 3 2 1
Year   2007 2006 2005 2004 2003

Cover photo from
Typeset by Fakenham Photosetting Limited Fakenham Norfolk
Printed in Great Britain for Hodder & Stoughton Educational, a division of Hodder Headline,
338 Euston Road, London NW1 3BH by The Bath Press Ltd, Bath.

Contents

1 Introduction

Destiny's Child began life
in Houston, Texas USA.

Lots of girls have been part of Destiny's Child.
Now there are just three.
Beyoncé Knowles,
Kelly Rowland and
Michelle Williams.

Destiny's Child have sold 30 million CDs.
They have had more US number ones
than any other girl band – ever.

They worked hard to get to the top.
There were setbacks on the way.

They have strong faith in God.
And that faith has given them hope.

2 Pretty Girls

Beyoncé Knowles
was born in September 1981.

Beyoncé was her mother's maiden name.
Her mum, Tina,
had been a singer in a local band.
Now she ran a beauty salon.

Beyoncé was shy
when she was little.
'It's hard being cute,
and having light skin,'
she says.

'And it's hard having a funny name!
People think you're so full of yourself!

Beyoncé with her sister, Solange.

'But I wasn't full of myself.
I was quiet and shy.
I didn't dare tell anyone
I could sing and dance!'

Then her dance teacher
entered her for a talent contest.
She was still only eight years old.
Beyoncé's mum and dad came to see her.
They knew she had talent
as soon as Beyoncé started to sing.

Beyoncé sees it another way:

'I didn't choose to be a singer,' she says.
'God put the talent in me.'

Beyoncé met up with two friends.
They were Kelly and LaTavia.

They sang in mum's beauty salon.
Dad, Mathew Knowles, started helping the girls.
He even gave up his job
to help the girls make a career.

When Kelly was six or seven,
her dad left home.
She never saw him again.
It was hard for Kelly's mum.

Kelly moved in with Beyoncé
and her mum and dad.
She was nine years old.
Beyoncé and Kelly
have lived together ever since.

3 Destiny

At first there were just the three girls.
Then there were four.

LeToya Luckett joined Beyoncé,
Kelly Rowland and LaTavia Roberson
in 1992.
(They were still only 11 years old!)

The group had lots of names
before they got the right one.

One day,
Beyoncé's mum was reading her Bible.
It fell open at a page,
and Tina read the word 'destiny'.
It was a short step from there
to the name Destiny's Child.

The four girls that made up the group between 1992 and 1998.

Beyoncé's dad Mathew
was the manager.
He got them a record deal.

But the deal fell through.

They were so young, says Beyoncé.
They were still only 15 or 16.

'The record company told me
to go away and get a personality!'

Destiny's Child soon bounced back.

They got a second record deal.
Their first single was 'Killing Time'.
It was used in the hit movie *Men In Black*.

Beyoncé with her dad.

The album *Destiny's Child*
came out in 1998.
The hit single 'No No No'
reached number 3 in the US charts.

The album sold over 300,000 copies
in three months.

The girls were only 16.
After eight years singing!
All the hard work
was just starting to pay off.

And then came a shock.

4 Then There Were Three

Things had not been right
with Destiny's Child for a while.

But it was still a shock
when LaTavia and LeToya left the group.
The girls had a tour to do.
They had an album to promote!

As the band found success,
the cracks started to show.

There were fights about money.
There were fights about Beyoncé.
How come she gets to sing all the songs?

And there were fights about Mathew.
He was their manager.
He was Beyoncé's dad.
He was Kelly's guardian.

LaTavia and LeToya said
he was greedy, and a control-freak.
They stood up to him.
Mathew froze them out.

'I turned on the TV,' says LaTavia.
'It was our new single,
'Say My Name'.
There were two new girls
in our places.
One of the new girls
was miming to my voice.

'That's how I knew
I was no longer in Destiny's Child!'

They all settled out of court.
But it took over two years to sort out.

For a while, Beyoncé took it all badly:

'I had just split up
with my boyfriend,'
she says.
'He'd been my boyfriend
since ninth grade.
Now I had no one to turn to.

'My skin was bad.
My hair was breaking off.
I was really stressing.

'What saved me was –
going to church.
God spoke to me
and I knew it was going to be okay.

'That was the happiest day of my life.'

Michelle also got stressed at this time.
She tells the story
of how she joined Destiny's Child:

'I was a backing singer in another band.
I had done some work with Destiny's Child.
We all got on really well.

'Then I got a phone call.
I went to the house
where Beyoncé and Kelly live
with their mum and dad.

'I sang for them,
and danced for them.
I stayed with them.
We had so much fun!'

Michelle Williams.

As Michelle was singing,
Beyoncé and Kelly looked at each other.
They were thinking:
she looks great.
She sounds great.
She wants to work really hard!
Thank God! We found her!
She's the one!

'A few days later,' Michelle goes on,
'I was miming to the video
of 'Say My Name'!

'A few days after that,
we were all at the Grammy Awards.
Then we went off on tour to Europe!
My feet didn't touch the ground!'

But the problems didn't end there.

A singer called Farrah Franklin
joined the group with Michelle.

After five months of non-stop work,
Farrah quit as well.

'We were at LA airport,' Beyoncé says.
'We were heading for Sydney, Australia.
We were all there – except Farrah.

'I called her.
She was still at home.
She wasn't coming to the airport.
She wasn't coming to Australia.
She wanted out.

'I spoke to Farrah for hours.
I told her – this is a job, like any other job.
You can't decide not to go,
just because you don't feel like it!'

Farrah was stressed.
She couldn't take the hard work.
Beyoncé, Kelly and Michelle
flew to Australia without her.

'At first, we were scared,' says Kelly.
'But then we prayed to God.
We worked harder on stage,
and changed our dance moves a bit.

'And as soon as we started to sing
we felt God on stage with us.
It was magic.
We sounded better than ever!
We knew we didn't have to look for anyone else.'

From now on,
Destiny's Child was just the three of them.
And it felt so right.

For Destiny's Child,
2000 and 2001 were great years.
In just over two years,
they did 200 concerts all over the world.

They won a handful of awards:
They were Artist of the Year
two years running!

The single 'Say My Name' was a big hit.
It won Best Single of the Year.
It also won Best Video of the Year.

The Writing's on the Wall
won Best R&B/Soul Album for 2000.
It sold over 130,000 in a week.
It went into the charts at number 6.
It went on to sell over ten million copies.

All the hard work had paid off!

What next for Destiny's Child?

Beyoncé says:
'We want to prove
that we're not just a pretty girl group.
Our next album will be full of surprises.
We want to surprise ourselves!
But we also want to try some solo projects.
We want to go it alone.'

5 Go It Alone

Michelle worked on a solo album.
It is called *Heart To Yours*.
It's deeper than Destiny's Child's albums.
More soul, less pop and R&B.

'I will be more covered up for a while!' she says.
'Less bare skin. More jackets, heels and hats!
That's more my style!'

Kelly has been working on a solo album too.
And she sang with Nelly
on his hit single – 'Dilemma'.
She's been getting into acting, too.

Beyoncé also acts.
She is the one with the big-screen career.

In 2002, Beyoncé starred in the movie
Austin Powers: Goldmember.
She played sexy Foxxy Cleopatra.
She helped Austin Powers
rid the world of Dr Evil.

'It's a comedy,' says Beyoncé.
'But I play a strong and sassy woman.
She's way over the top.
She still has a lot of soul.
She's cool. I can relate to her.'

'It can be hard for a singer
to get into acting,' she says.
'People are ready to put you down.
Look at Cher. Look at Madonna.

'I work extra hard.
I have to be extra good.
Then people take me seriously.
It's a challenge.
But I like a challenge!'

Beyoncé must have done something right.
Goldmember took over 71 million dollars
in its first weekend in the United States!

Beyoncé as Foxxy Cleopatra in *Austin Powers: Goldmember*.

6 Thanks to God

Life on the road is hard.
The days are long.
You are always on the go.
You never get enough sleep.
Where do the girls get their energy?

Kelly has the answer:
'I pray to God – every day.'

'When I have a problem,'
Michelle says,
'I ask God for help. For advice.
He always makes things right.
He never lets me down.'

'We may be stars,' says Beyoncé.
'We may have a video on MTV.
But we are only human.
We have our ups and downs.'

7 Independent Women

'People think we live in Barbie World,'
says Beyoncé.
'But we don't.
No way am I a living doll!'

The 2002 hit single
says it all:

'Independent Women part 1'
is about strong women,
who don't depend on anyone.
They work hard for what they want.
They pay their way
with their own money.

It was a strong song.
It was on the movie soundtrack
for *Charlie's Angels*.

'Bills Bills Bills' is another strong song.
It's about dropping boyfriends.
Boyfriends who don't pay their way.
Boyfriends who try to control you.

'I like to look on the bright side,' Beyoncé says.
'Good songs can come out of bad relationships!'

And where did 'Survivor' come from?

'Some guy said
being in Destiny's Child must be like
being in a reality-TV *Survivor* show.

'That made me so angry!' says Beyoncé.
'So I turned it round.
Destiny's Child have had our problems,
but we are strong women.
We have survived!'

Destiny's Child at the Grammy Awards, 2002.

Beyoncé writes most of the songs
for Destiny's Child.
She's also into yoga and oil painting.
There's also that solo album.
There's also the star-studded movie career.

It all shows there's more to her
than just a pretty face.
So – is there talk of a solo career
for Beyoncé?

She says no:

'If the solo projects all go badly,
there will <u>always</u> be Destiny's Child.

'And if the solo projects go really well,'
she adds,
'there will <u>still</u> be Destiny's Child!'